Skateboards:

Designs and Equipment

By B. A. Hoena

Content Consultant:
Pete Connelly
Staff writer, *Heckler* magazine

CAPSTONE
HIGH-INTEREST
BOOKS

an imprint of Capstone Press
Mankato, Minnesota

Capstone High-Interest Books are published by Capstone Press
151 Good Counsel Drive, P.O. Box 669, Mankato, Minnesota 56002
http://www.capstone-press.com

Library of Congress Cataloging-in-Publication Data
Hoena, B. A.
    Skateboards : designs and equipment/by B.A. Hoena.
    p. cm.—(Skateboarding)
    Includes bibliographical references and index.
    Summary: Describes the changes in skateboards throughout the history of
the sport, discussing essential gear as well.
    ISBN 0-7368-1073-0
    1. Skateboards—History—Juvenile literature. 2. Skateboards—Equipment
and supplies—Juvenile literature. [1. Skateboarding—History.] I. Title.
II. Series.
GV859.8 .H64 2002
688.7'622—dc21
                                                                  2001003923

Editorial Credits
Angela Kaelberer, editor; Timothy Halldin, cover designer, interior layout
    designer, and interior illustrator; Katy Kudela, photo researcher

Photo Credits
AP/Wide World Photos, 8, 14
Capstone Press/Gary Sundermeyer, 7, 10, 12–13, 17, 19, 20, 23, 28;
    Jim Foell, 24, 26
Hulton/Archive Photos, 4
Patrick Batchelder, cover

**Capstone Press thanks Adam Dagsgard and the skaters of Burnsville
Skate Park in Burnsville, Minnesota; the staff and skaters of John Rose
OVAL in Roseville, Minnesota; and In the Works Skate Supply and Ernie
November Records of Mankato, Minnesota, for their assistance with
this book.**

1 2 3 4 5 6 07 06 05 04 03 02

Table of Contents

Kids made early skateboards from scooters.

Development of the Skateboard

In the early 1950s, kids started tearing the uprights off their scooters. The kids then had a wooden board with roller skate wheels nailed to the bottom. At the time, these skaters had no idea that they had just invented skateboarding. They were just kids trying to have fun.

Learn About

- The first skateboards
- Skateboard parts
- Early skateboards

Skateboard Parts

A skateboard has three main parts. These parts are the deck, the trucks, and the wheels.

Skaters stand on the skateboard's deck. The front of the deck is called the nose. The back is called the tail. The tail curves up. The curved area is called a kicktail. Skaters use the kicktail to perform tricks.

Parts called trucks connect the wheels to the bottom of the board. Each skateboard has two trucks.

Trucks are made of aluminum. This strong, lightweight metal allows the trucks to withstand the shock from bumps.

Skaters can choose from wheels of different sizes and levels of hardness. The wheels skaters choose depend on the type of skating they do.

Early Skateboards

The first skateboards had a simple design. They had metal wheels. The boards did not grip the riding

Skateboards have a deck, trucks, and wheels.

surface well. Skaters also had a hard time making the boards turn.

In the late 1950s, many surfers began skateboarding. Skateboarding soon became known as "sidewalk surfing." Skateboarding equipment improved as the sport became more popular.

1980s ramp skaters used large, wide boards.

CHAPTER TWO

Decks

Decks also are called boards or planks. The shape and size of decks has changed over the years. In the 1960s, boards were short and narrow. In the 1970s, many skaters rode in empty swimming pools. These skaters found that longer boards were better for pool riding.

In the 1980s, skaters rode on large ramps shaped like the letter "U." These ramps are called half-pipes or vert ramps. Ramp skaters used long, wide boards. Some of these boards were as wide as 12 inches (30 centimeters).

Learn About

- Pool and ramp riders
- Deck material
- Board size

Skaters often skate at high speeds on ramps.

Today's Boards

By the 1990s, street skating was popular. Street skaters perform tricks using obstacles often found on or near city streets. These obstacles include curbs, handrails, and benches.

Street skaters used boards that were 7 to 8.5 inches (18 to 22 centimeters) wide. These boards had a kicktail on the nose as well as the tail. Today, many boards have double kicktails.

Decks are made from several thin layers of wood. The layers are pressed and glued together. The layers make the decks strong enough to be used for tricks. Most skaters consider maple to be the best wood for decks.

Skater Preference

Street skaters use boards that are about 32 inches (81 centimeters) long and about 7.5 inches (19 centimeters) wide. Wide decks are easier for skaters to balance on as they perform tricks.

Ramp and pool skaters also use boards about 32 inches (81 centimeters) long. But their boards usually are wider than street skaters' boards. Ramp and pool skaters use boards that are between 7.5 and 9 inches (19 and 23 centimeters) wide. Ramp and pool skaters usually skate at higher speeds than street skaters. The wider boards give ramp and pool skaters a steadier surface on which to balance.

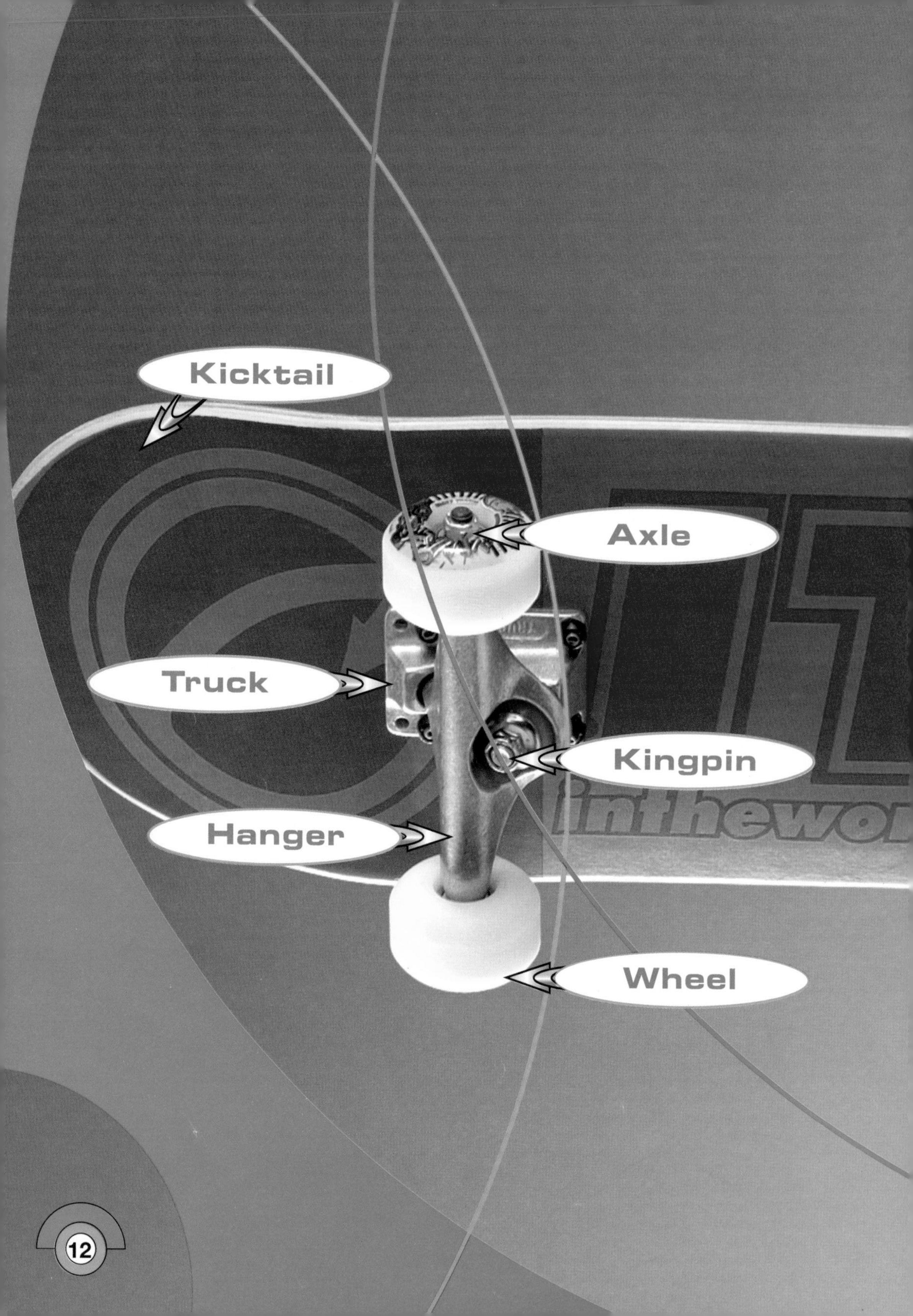

Kicktail

Axle

Truck

Kingpin

Hanger

Wheel

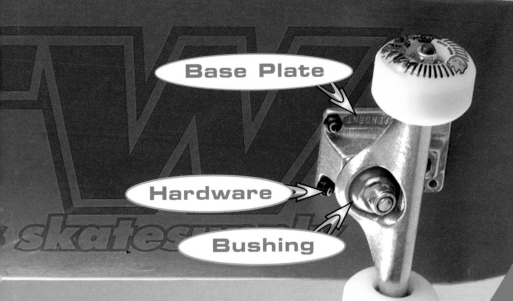

Deck

Base Plate

Hardware

Bushing

Skateboard wheels changed in the 1970s.

CHAPTER THREE

Wheels and Trucks

Baked clay wheels replaced metal roller skate wheels in the early 1960s. Clay wheels cost less and had a smoother ride than metal wheels. But they also wore out more quickly.

In 1972, skater Frank Nasworthy started selling wheels made of polyurethane. This rubberlike material often is called "urethane."

Urethane wheels quickly became popular. The wheels make less noise and grip pavement better than clay wheels. Urethane wheels also last longer than clay wheels.

Learn About

- Wheel material
- Wheel size and durometer
- Trucks

Wheel Size

Wheels can be different widths and diameters. Diameter is the height of a wheel. Wheel size is measured in millimeters. The average wheel is 20 to 30 millimeters wide and 45 to 66 millimeters in diameter.

The size of wheels skaters use depends on the type of skating that they do. Many ramp skaters use narrow wheels. Wide wheels grip surfaces well and give skaters more control during turns. But wide wheels create more friction because more of the wheel's surface touches the pavement. Friction slows down skateboards.

Many ramp skaters also use wheels with a large diameter. Boards with these wheels can travel at faster speeds than those with small-diameter wheels. Ramp skaters use wheels as large as 66 millimeters in diameter.

Wheels can be different widths and diameters.

Wheels with small diameters are slower than large-diameter wheels. But they also are lightweight. Lighter wheels move easier than heavier wheels. For example, street skaters use small wheels to perform tricks such as flips. These wheels are as small as 45 millimeters in diameter.

Durometer

A wheel's hardness is measured in durometer. Most skateboard wheels have a durometer between 78 and 101. Harder wheels have a higher durometer.

Skaters choose wheel hardness based on the type of skating they do. Most ramp and street skaters use wheels with a durometer of 97 to 100.

Truck Parts

Each truck has several parts. The hanger connects the wheels to the truck. The hanger is a large piece of metal with a round hole drilled through it. A metal rod called an axle fits inside this hole. The wheels attach to each end of the axle. Bearings fit between the wheels and the axle. These small metal balls reduce the friction between the axle and the wheels.

A flat metal plate called a base plate connects the truck to the board. Four screws fasten the base plate to the board. These screws are called hardware.

Street skaters use wheels with a
durometer of 97 to 100.

A part called a kingpin connects the hanger
to the base plate. Skaters can loosen or tighten
the kingpin. A loose kingpin allows the board
to turn easily. Street skaters prefer loose
kingpins. Ramp skaters tighten their kingpins
to make the boards steadier.

Truck size is measured by hanger width.

Trivia

In 2001, the International Association of Skateboard Companies said that at least 20 million people in the world are skaters. Skateboard companies make about 100,000 new skateboards each month.

Bushings

Round pieces of urethane rest on the kingpin between the hanger and base plate. These pieces are called bushings. They allow the truck to turn smoothly.

Bushings come in different durometers. A harder durometer makes the truck stiffer and harder to turn. A softer durometer allows the truck to turn quickly.

Truck Size and Wheelbase

Truck size is measured by hanger width. This width is measured in millimeters. Trucks are available in sizes from 101 millimeters to 215 millimeters. Most skaters use trucks that are between 135 and 155 millimeters.

The distance between the front and rear trucks is called the wheelbase. Most street skaters prefer a short wheelbase. Skateboards with a short wheelbase turn easily. Ramp skaters prefer a long wheelbase. The long wheelbase makes the skateboard steadier.

Truck History

Early trucks did not allow skaters to turn easily. Skaters loosened the trucks' hardware to allow the trucks to turn. But loose trucks made boards unsteady and unsafe.

In the 1970s, skateboard companies developed new trucks that allowed some turns. But skaters wanted boards that could make wider and sharper turns.

In 1978, a company called Ermico Enterprises changed skateboarding forever. This company invented a new type of truck called the Independent Suspension truck.

The Independent Suspension truck has a base plate and a hanger. The base plate and the hanger allow skaters to turn by shifting their weight from heel to toe. Skaters still use Independent Suspension trucks today.

Independent Suspension trucks still are made today.

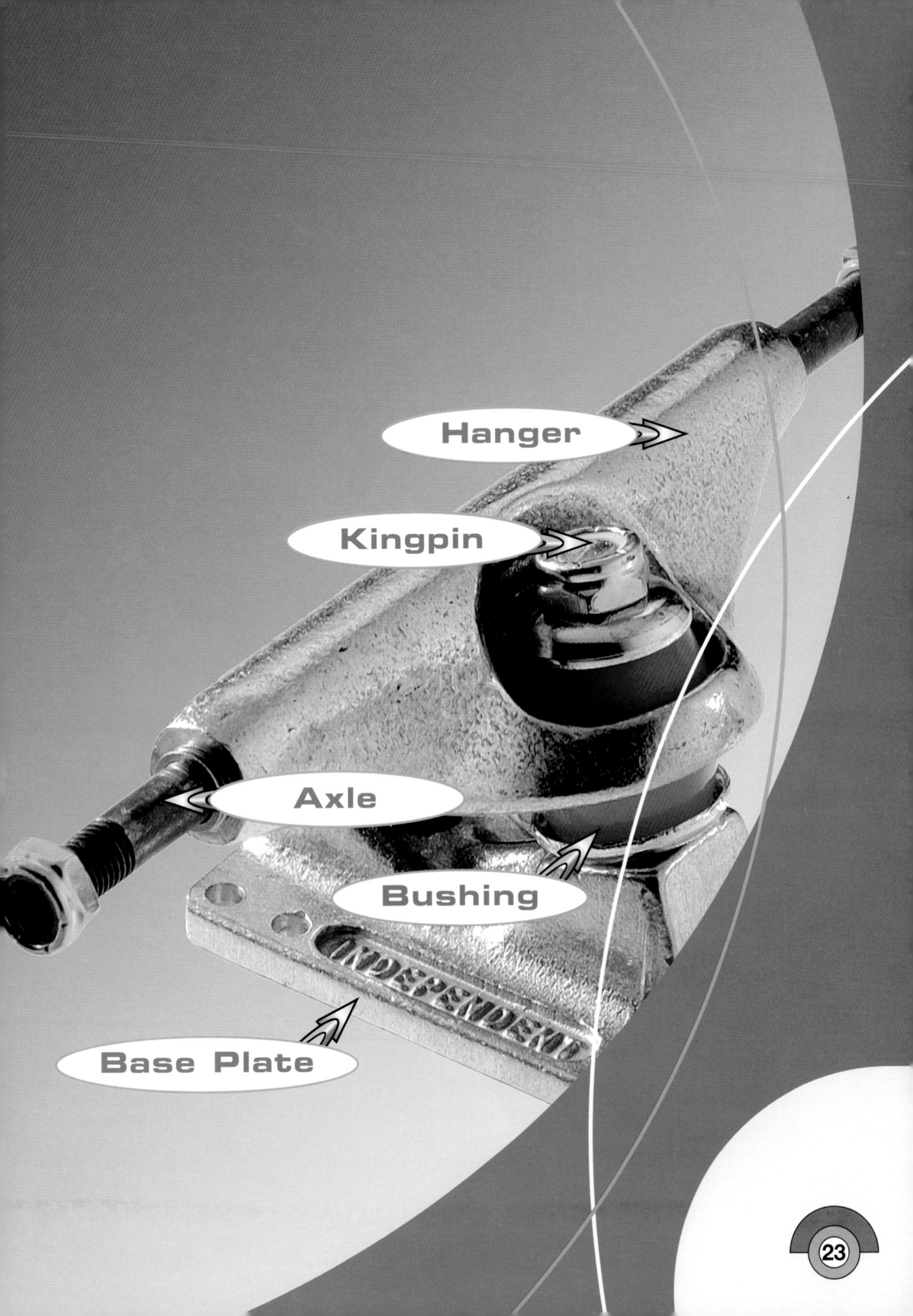

Hanger

Kingpin

Axle

Bushing

Base Plate

INDEPENDENT

Skaters should take care of their boards.

Skateboarding Gear

Skaters often brag about their road rash and raspberries. But skaters can receive more serious injuries than scrapes and bruises. Skaters who wear the proper clothing and safety equipment can protect themselves from these injuries.

Skaters also should keep their boards in good working order. Skaters should be sure that their trucks' hardware is properly tightened. They should make sure that the wheels spin. They also should check for cracks in their decks.

Learn About

- Board maintenance
- Protective gear
- Clothing

Skaters should wear protective gear.

Trivia In the 1960s, skaters glued sand to the top of their decks. The sand allowed their feet to better grip the board. Today, skaters put strips of grip tape on the top of their decks. Grip tape is made of material that feels similar to sandpaper. It helps skaters better control their boards.

Protective Gear

Falls on pavement and concrete can cause painful injuries. Skaters wear several types of protective gear to help prevent injuries.

All skaters should wear helmets. Helmets protect skaters from injuries such as concussions. A blow to the head causes these brain injuries.

Skaters also should wear knee and elbow pads. Skaters often fall on their knees and elbows. Some ramp skaters also wear knee gaskets. Skaters wear these pads under their kneepads. Knee gaskets help the kneepads stay in place when skaters sweat.

Many skaters wear gloves and wrist guards. Wrist guards have a plastic brace. This brace holds the wrist straight. This position can prevent the wrist from breaking during a fall.

Clothing

Skaters need proper shoes. Many skaters wear high-top sneakers. These shoes support skaters' ankles. Most skateboarding shoes have soft soles. These soles allow skaters to better feel the skateboard.

Skaters also should wear protective clothing. Long-sleeved shirts and denim pants protect skaters' skin during falls.

Skaters who wear protective gear and take care of their equipment are less likely to be injured. Healthy skaters can improve both their skills and their sport.

Denim pants protect skaters' skin during falls.

Words to Know

axle (AK-suhl)—a rod in the center of a wheel; the wheel turns around the axle.

bearing (BAIR-ing)—a small metal ball between a wheel and an axle

diameter (dye-AM-uh-tur)—the height of a skateboard wheel

durometer (duh-RAH-muh-tur)—the measurement of a skateboard wheel's hardness

friction (FRIK-shuhn)—the force produced when two objects rub against each other; friction slows down objects.

polyurethane (pah-lee-YUR-uh-thayn)—a hard, rubberlike plastic used to make skateboard wheels

To Learn More

Burke, L. M. *Skateboarding! Surf the Pavement.* The Extreme Sports Collection. New York: Rosen Publishing, 1999.

Freimuth, Jeri. *Extreme Skateboarding Moves.* Behind the Moves. Mankato, Minn.: Capstone High-Interest Books, 2001.

Maurer, Tracy Nelson. *Skateboarding.* Radsports Guides. Vero Beach, Fla.: Rourke, 2001.

Useful Addresses

International Association of Skateboard Companies
P. O. Box 37
Santa Barbara, CA 93116

Transworld Skateboarding Magazine
353 Airport Road
Oceanside, CA 92054

Internet Sites

Skateboard.com
http://www.skateboard.com

Skateboard Science Exploratorium
http://www.exploratorium.edu/skateboarding

**Skatepark Association of the United States
of America**
http://www.spausa.org

Index